SEXISM AT WORK

BY DUCHESS HARRIS, JD, PHD
WITH GAIL RADLEY

Essential Library

An Imprint of Abdo Publishing | abdopublishing.com

ABDOPUBLISHING.COM

Published by Abdo Publishing, a division of ABDO, PO Box 398166, Minneapolis, Minnesota 55439. Copyright © 2018 by Abdo Consulting Group, Inc. International copyrights reserved in all countries. No part of this book may be reproduced in any form without written permission from the publisher. Essential Library™ is a trademark and logo of Abdo Publishing.

Printed in the United States of America, North Mankato, Minnesota
092017
012018

THIS BOOK CONTAINS RECYCLED MATERIALS

Cover Photo: Shutterstock Images
Interior Photos: Cecilie Arcurs/iStockphoto, 4–5; Jerome A. Pollos/Coeur d'Alene Press/AP Images, 8; Kevin Dietsch/UPI/Newscom, 10–11; Everett Collection/Newscom, 14–15; Everett-Art/Shutterstock Images, 17; World History Archives/Newscom, 19; Underwood Archives/UIG Universal Images Group/Newscom, 23; iStockphoto, 26–27, 57, 60, 68, 80; Monkey Business Images/Shutterstock Images, 30, 77; Erik McGregor/Pacific Press/Newscom, 34–35; Art Wager/iStockphoto, 38; Mark Ralston/Reuters/Newscom, 41; David Zalubowski/AP Images, 44–45; Andrey Popov/Shutterstock Images, 50; Shutterstock Images, 52–53, 78 (top right), 78 (middle left), 78 (bottom right), 78 (bottom left); Erik McGregor/Sipa USA/Newscom, 62–63; Hybrid Images/iStockphoto, 67; Monkey Business Images/iStockphoto, 72; Richard Drew/AP Images, 74–75; Rashad Ashurov/Shutterstock Images, 78 (top left); Romuald Meigneux/Sipa/Newscom, 84 (top); Rob Crandall/Shutterstock Images, 84 (bottom); Chad Harder/AP Images, 85 (top); NASA/Notimex/Newscom, 85 (bottom); Fang Xia Nuo/iStockphoto, 86–87; Katarzyna Bialasiewicz/iStockphoto, 90; Steve Debenport/iStockphoto, 92–93; Syda Productions/Shutterstock Images, 98

Editor: Alyssa Krekelberg
Series Designer: Maggie Villaume

PUBLISHER'S CATALOGING-IN-PUBLICATION DATA

Names: Harris, Duchess, author | Radley, Gail, author.
Title: Sexism at work / by Duchess Harris and Gail Radley.
Description: Minneapolis, Minnesota : Abdo Publishing, 2018. | Series: Being female in America |
Identifiers: LCCN 2017946733 | ISBN 9781532113093 (lib.bdg.) | ISBN 9781532151972 (ebook)
Subjects: LCSH: Sexism--Juvenile literature. | Discrimination in employment--Juvenile literature. | Social history--Juvenile literature.
Classification: DDC 331.4--dc23
LC record available at https://lccn.loc.gov/2017946733

CONTENTS

CHAPTER ONE

A PERSISTENT PROBLEM

Cynthia Haddad's goal of becoming a pharmacist began when she was in eighth grade, and she never let it go. The dream carried her through years of schooling and to the Wal-Mart pharmacy in Pittsfield, Massachusetts, that hired her in 1993.

Haddad did her job well. Nine years of excellent work reviews stacked up, filled with comments such as "a huge asset to the department" and "very reliable." She had "done a great job keeping the department together," one review noted.[1] Her career was taking off when, in 2003, Wal-Mart made her temporary manager of the pharmacy. Her temporary position stretched on for approximately 13 months, with Haddad performing all the duties of a permanent manager. Then she was fired.

What happened? Haddad had discovered that male pharmacists earned more than she did and that they were given bonuses she never received. After filling the manager's role for nine months, Haddad raised the issue with her supervisor. At first, her complaint seemed to make no difference; then Wal-Mart cut a bonus check for those nine months of work. But Haddad didn't drop the issue because Wal-Mart still hadn't addressed the problem of the pay difference. She wondered why she was paid less than other pharmacists. So Wal-Mart issued a second bonus and, five days afterward, in April 2004, fired her.

In explanation for her dismissal, Wal-Mart accused Haddad of leaving the pharmacy attended by a pharmacy technician. During that time, Wal-Mart said the technician logged into the computer using Haddad's credentials and issued himself a prescription, an ulcer medication called Prevacid.

A distraught Haddad confined herself to her house for the next six months. She worried that she would never work as a pharmacist again. To save her reputation, Haddad, a mother of four, hired lawyers and took her case to court. Three years later, at trial, the truth came out. The Prevacid theft had happened 18 months *before* she was fired. At that time,

WAL-MART SUPPORTS WOMEN'S BUSINESSES

Similar to most businesses, Wal-Mart's official policies seek to advance women in the workplace, and recent actions support that claim. In March 2017, Wal-Mart pledged to publicly report on its efforts to obtain products from female-owned businesses. It facilitated the participation of eight other large companies in the Women's Business Enterprise National Council initiative. This effort follows a five-year international program in which Wal-Mart gave training to approximately one million women and expanded its purchases from female-owned businesses.[2] "Creating economic opportunity and growth is central to who we are as a company," commented president and CEO of Wal-Mart, Doug McMillon. "We are proud to be part of this important initiative, and together we can make an even bigger impact in elevating these successful women-owned businesses."[3]

Pharmacy technicians assist pharmacists in collecting the medicine for patients' prescriptions.

Haddad reported the missing drugs to the federal Drug Enforcement Administration as required. Apparently satisfied, Wal-Mart promoted her to temporary manager after the unauthorized prescription incident. One male witness, also a former Wal-Mart pharmacist, testified that a technician had stolen the narcotic painkiller Vicodin under his watch, and not only was the pharmacist not penalized, but the technician was not fired. Instead, the technician was allowed to quit, leaving his record unblemished. Furthermore, Massachusetts had no law against pharmacists leaving the pharmacy and its technicians unsupervised for brief periods. In fact, it was common practice. It seemed to Haddad and her lawyers that Wal-Mart was more concerned with Haddad's insistence on equal treatment than with missing drugs or unguarded pharmacies.

The jury agreed with Haddad: Wal-Mart had tarnished Haddad's reputation without cause. However, the jury didn't require the company to pay for that offense. It did demand that Wal-Mart pay Haddad $1 million as punishment for the offense and another $1 million in lost pay, emotional trauma, and medical expenses. "My story was told and I did the fight," Haddad commented. Hearing that the jury agreed with her, she said, "started to bring the life back into me. Someone listened."[4]

VARIETIES OF UNEQUAL TREATMENT

Although women outnumber men as pharmacists, the pay difference continues. Whether

ALTARS TO EQUALITY?

Business and economics writer Jordan Weissmann says that pharmacies have become "little altars to gender equality."[5] He pointed out that most pharmacies were once independently owned by male pharmacists. As drugstore chains began to dot the landscape, standard pay scales that didn't take gender into account were established. The chain stores also offered more opportunities to work part-time, appealing to those with childcare responsibilities. Women noticed and headed into pharmacy schools. According to Claudia Goldin, a Harvard economist, as of 2014, the pay gap between men and women working as pharmacists had shrunk to between 5 and 7 percent.[6]

Betty Dukes, *left*, filed a sex discrimination lawsuit against Wal-Mart in 2000. As a Wal-Mart employee for six years, Dukes claimed she never received opportunities for promotions like her male coworkers.

it's pay difference or another variety of unequal treatment, lawsuits continue to plague pharmacies.

In 2013, pharmacist Arian Lemon found herself without a job. In the same month her pharmacy technician, Emilee Stephens, was also let go from her position. What else did the two women have in common? Both were pregnant, and both had received disparaging comments about their pregnancies from the pharmacy's owner. In 2016, the court directed the company to pay

the two women $85,000, to be divided between them, for pregnancy discrimination.[7]

Another court case occurred after a New Hampshire Wal-Mart pharmacist, Maureen McPadden, was fired because she lost her store key. However, she pointed out that a male pharmacist had also lost his key and kept his job. McPadden believed her dismissal had more to do with her gender and that she had reported safety and privacy problems at the pharmacy. She believed that her taking two weeks off, as allowed by the Family and Medical

Leave Act, also figured into the company's decision. In her 2016 trial, the jury agreed with McPadden and required Wal-Mart to pay her $31.2 million, of which $15 million was a gender discrimination penalty.[8] However, the judge later reduced the total to approximately $16 million, arguing that both the amount intended to punish Wal-Mart and the back pay award were too high.[9]

LINGERING ATTITUDES

These cases of gender discrimination encountered in the pharmacies are not unique. Similar problems crop up in diverse workplaces across the country. Although such problems persist, women have made great strides in the fight for their rights. But lingering attitudes and discriminatory practices continue to affect their opportunities and experiences, no matter their type of employment.

Sexual harassment is a display of power relations. Because of sexist practices in the workplace, women

NUMBERS AT THE EEOC

The United States Equal Employment Opportunity Commission (EEOC), launched in 1964, is the agency charged with making sure federal laws against discrimination are followed. Thousands of cases are referred to the EEOC for investigation each year. The EEOC tries to settle these cases with the disputing parties. When it cannot, the parties may proceed to a lawsuit. In 1997, 30.7 percent of the cases reported were related to sex discrimination. By 2016, that number had risen to 35.3 percent, or nearly 27,000 cases.[10]

are less likely to hold power and are therefore more likely to be sexually harassed. High-profile cases of sexual harassment on the job and discriminatory hiring practices are frequently reported in the news. Sometimes, though, discrimination occurs without the person even recognizing it. Unless a woman knows her male counterpart's credentials and experience, she may not realize she is being passed over for a job based on gender. If she doesn't know his salary, she may not realize hers is lower. But, because of antidiscrimination laws, much sexist treatment comes in subtler forms, such as comments that seem a little too personal and gender based, choice projects being handed to other workers, or demeaning comments. Legal equality is a vital step, but laws alone don't eliminate sexist attitudes and unconscious practices.

DISCUSSION STARTERS

- Why do you believe people discriminate against women in the workplace? Do you think their discriminatory actions are intentional?
- What steps should people take if they are being treated unfairly because of their gender?
- While laws can't force changes in attitudes, do they help? How? What else does it take to change attitudes?

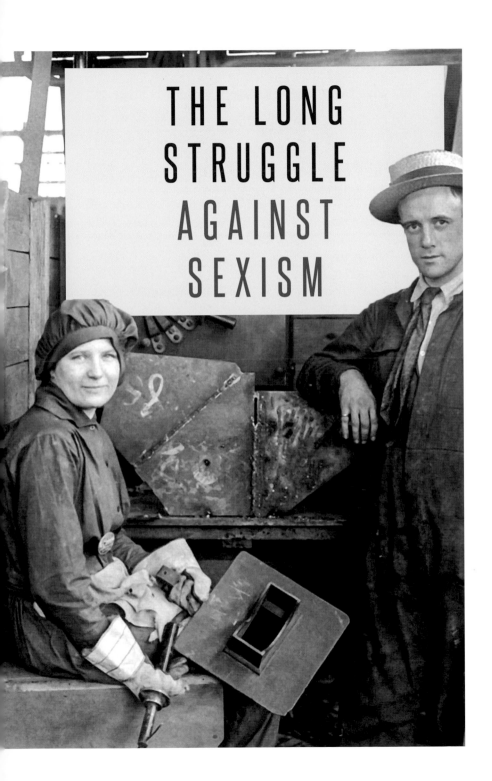

CHAPTER TWO

THE LONG STRUGGLE AGAINST SEXISM

Sexist attitudes toward women were generally absent among the country's first inhabitants, the Native Americans. Though women's roles might have differed from men's, women had power and respect in most communities. Some, such as Shawnee, Cherokee, and Iroquois women, chose tribal leaders or became leaders themselves. But early American settlers brought their own beliefs about women and women's roles with them from Europe.

Some determined European women did manage to influence their husbands and participate more fully in the growing nation. Abigail Adams, for example, ran her family's farm and dairy businesses during the lengthy absences of her husband John, a Founding Father and later the second president of the

THE POWERFUL NATIVE AMERICAN WOMEN

In colonial times, Native Americans lived by their own laws and customs. Native American women cared for children and prepared meals. But in some tribes, such as the Cherokee, land passed from mother to daughter. Iroquois women also exercised control over tribal land, making decisions about crops and affecting their community's economy in other ways. Women were also valued in many tribes for medical skills and spiritual leadership. However, Native American women's status weakened when the US government passed the 1887 Dawes Act, which divided native land among the men. The Indian Reorganization Act of 1934 did even more damage. While supporters hoped to restore Native Americans' right to govern themselves, the act replaced the tribes' more egalitarian governmental systems with a male-centered one, depriving women of their ability to choose leaders.

Abigail Adams didn't have a formal education, but she was an avid reader.

United States. She frequently gave her husband advice in wise, well-informed letters. In an often-quoted message dated March 31, 1776, she followed a plea for women with a warning:

> *I desire you would Remember the Ladies, and be more generous and favorable to them than were your ancestors. Do not put such unlimited power into the hands of the Husbands. Remember all Men would be tyrants if they could. If particular care and attention are not paid to the Ladies, we are determined to foment a Rebellion, and will not hold ourselves bound by any Laws in which we have no voice or Representation.[1]*

Usually, though, women couldn't venture far from home and family for their work and influence. Most people believed women were meant to obey and serve their husbands and should have limited rights.

EXPANDING ROLES

As the country grew, domestic work and schoolteaching became acceptable employment outside the home, particularly for unmarried white women. When factories and mills appeared in the early 1800s, more of these women found ways to earn a salary. Enslaved African-American women had always been forced to work at least as hard as the men. However, wealthy white women were considered too delicate for such activity. They were expected to refrain from even labor at home. It wasn't until 1920 that women won the right to vote throughout the country, after decades of political activism for the cause. But beliefs in women's inferiority to men persisted.

However, war brought women greater freedom to take on nontraditional roles. Thousands of men left their jobs to fight in World War I

SENECA FALLS CONVENTION

The country's first women's rights convention took place in the summer of 1848 in Seneca Falls, New York. Hundreds of attendees debated the Declaration of Principles, which organizers had patterned after the Declaration of Independence. Although activist Elizabeth Cady Stanton's dream of demanding the right to vote was narrowly vetoed by the convention, the remaining principles passed. One of them related to freedom of employment.

The Rosie the Riveter poster was used as a recruitment tool to encourage women to join the workforce.

(1914–1918) and World War II (1939–1945). Other jobs that were directly related to the war effort, such as airplane and ammunition manufacturing, were looking for employees. A campaign praising the fictional Rosie the Riveter welcomed women into these roles during World War II. But female workers still earned less than males doing the same work. And when the wars ended, the men came home ready to fill those positions. It was no longer patriotic for women to work. They were pressured to step aside for the men.

Women were reluctant to give up their work positions and earnings. And women of color seldom had the luxury of choosing a life devoted entirely to their own homes and families, before or after the wars. Because of widespread discrimination against people of color, few families could get along on just one income. It often took the efforts of both husband and wife to scrape together enough money to support the family.

Although women were forced back into so-called pink-collar jobs, millions continued to work outside the home. Feminists pushed forward various proposals for equal pay and opportunities. The most well-known proposal was the Equal Rights Amendment (ERA), which was first introduced in 1923. The ERA promised full gender equality throughout the country. It was designed to protect gender rights not specifically addressed in the Constitution, such as the right to vote and protection against sex discrimination. However, the ERA did not receive enough support to pass.

ADVANCES IN THE 1960s

In the 1960s, a push for progress gained momentum. In 1963, President John F. Kennedy's Commission on the Status of Women issued its report, *American Women*. The report advocated for equal opportunity and pay for women, affordable childcare, support for homemakers, more varied job training, and other benefits. The report brought together a team of people with common concerns who would continue to advocate on women's behalf. State commissions to investigate women's statuses were established, eventually leading to the founding of the National Organization of Women (NOW), a group that would be pivotal in carrying forward the movement for women's rights.

Unfortunately, the commission was not as helpful concerning women of color, despite African-American women being consulted by the commission. Many African-American women were hopeful that when the report was released it would address the way race and gender work together to handicap black women in the workplace. For example, few black women were hired as secretaries because many secretarial schools were segregated. Subcommittees recommended training programs to promote advancement and rights and protections for domestic workers.

NATIONAL ORGANIZATION OF WOMEN

Founded in 1966, the National Organization of Women (NOW) is the premier women's rights organization. It has attracted women of every race and boasts many thousands of members throughout the country. The organization cites six issues as being its primary focus: reproductive rights and justice; ending violence against women; economic justice; lesbian, gay, bisexual, transgender, and queer rights; racial justice; and a Constitutional Equality Amendment. The amendment is an effort to guarantee full equality in all levels of society through the Constitution, rather than by laws that can be easily repealed.

Vocational guidance programs for black youth were another important proposal, intended to counteract the tendency of teachers, guidance counselors, and others to steer them toward unskilled and low-skilled jobs. But when the final commission report was released, it did not include the subcommittees' recommendations.

Meanwhile, the civil rights movement was gaining momentum. Many women lent their energies to that cause. In some cases, gains for people of color were also gains for women, such as when sex discrimination was added to the Civil Rights Act, passed in 1964. The addition of sex discrimination to the Civil Rights Act made it illegal to discriminate based on gender, just as it was illegal to do so based on race. But some female civil rights workers found themselves second class within the movement. For example, male members of some groups assumed women would undertake traditionally female tasks such as secretarial work. Some women were excluded from leadership roles and ignored in decision-making. Some endured sexual harassment and other abuses.

SECOND WAVE FEMINISM

Women took what they learned about activism in civil rights to launch what came to be called Second Wave

The Women's Caucus of Youth Against War and Fascism held a campaign for equal rights in the 1970s.

Feminism or the Women's Liberation Movement. Groups formed to help women understand the ways society had shaped their expectations and narrowed their opportunities. The new women's rights groups reignited the battle over passage of the ERA. The amendment finally passed in Congress in 1972. However, the states failed to pass it, so it did not become part of the Constitution.

As the 1970s unfolded, more women earned university and college degrees, took newly created women's studies courses, and joined the workforce than ever before. However, once in the workforce, many women experienced continued discrimination, pay imbalances, and sexual harassment. These problems were often viewed as coming with the territory, and many believed women should resolve these issues themselves, often by quitting their jobs. But one very public case caught the country's attention and educated the public about sexual harassment.

In 1991, President George H. W. Bush nominated Clarence Thomas to the Supreme Court. During the hearings, attorney Anita Hill, a former employee of Thomas's, claimed he had repeatedly sexually harassed her. Both Thomas and Hill were black, and interest in a case involving two African Americans was high. Hill was accused of sexual fantasizing, outright lying, and seeking revenge after a rebuff by Thomas. Feminists lined up behind Hill. They saw no reason why Hill would subject herself to such public examination if her claims weren't true.

ADVERTISEMENTS: "GIRL WANTED"

Employment advertisements in newspapers once directed female readers to jobs traditionally held by women through wording such as "Help Wanted Female." The advertisements often indicated how these potential employees would be treated. Ads calling for "Gal Friday," or a "one girl office" and "attractive ladies" were common.[2] In 1973, years of NOW picketing newspaper offices paid off when the Supreme Court narrowly determined gender-segregated ads to be discriminatory.

Thomas won the argument—and his seat on the Supreme Court—but a national conversation on sexual harassment had begun. Six weeks later, thousands of people raised funds to run an ad in *Time* magazine supporting the defeated Hill. The powerful statement brought focus to the stereotyping and silence of black women, who had often faced sexual harassment, abuse, and assault, beginning with the days of slavery. It responded to Thomas's characterization of Hill's accusations and the hearings that followed as "a high-tech lynching" as being done to deflect "attention away from the reality of sexual abuse in African American women's lives."[3] The widely publicized statement helped develop public understanding of the intersection of racism and sexism and the need for gender equality.

DISCUSSION STARTERS

- What concerns might people have had about the changing role of women? Are these still issues today?

- How do you think women felt about the conflicting messages about work they got before and after the World Wars? What do such messages say to women about their abilities and purpose?

- Many people in the United States followed the Hill-Thomas controversy. Why do you think this was?

CHAPTER THREE

IMPACT OF STEREOTYPES

"Sugar and spice and all that's nice—that's what little girls are made of!"[1] So goes the old nursery rhyme. Although it's not scientific, it appears complimentary. Unfortunately, the meaning behind it is quite different. The chant reveals the sort of thinking that has impacted women through the ages: women and girls are made differently and so must act and be treated differently. This type of thinking impacted Lorena Weeks in 1966, when she was denied the opportunity to be a switchman for Southern Bell Telephone Company. She had been working for the company since 1947, so she figured she deserved consideration for the position. Along with other benefits, the job would mean a higher salary. But the job was intended for men, she was told; it required the worker to lift 30 pounds (14 kg).[2] The company may have thought it was protecting women, but women routinely carry groceries and children weighing more. Even Weeks' typewriter, which she toted from place to place at work, weighed more.

INTERPRETING BEHAVIORS

The same behavior shown by men and women can be interpreted differently. When a man demonstrates a decisive, take-charge attitude, he might be described as a good leader or an effective boss, while the woman might be considered bossy. A man working late is likely regarded as committed to the job, while a woman might be suspected of neglecting her family.

It took years of appeals, but Weeks finally won her battle and got the job.

The stereotypes about women involve more than physical abilities. For example, girls have traditionally been steered toward careers that involve children, such as teaching and day care work. Many are also encouraged to enter caregiving fields, such as nursing and social work. Boys, on the other hand, are steered toward fields such as medicine, law, engineering, and business.

However, one study involving male and female business school students showed that both sexes had strong managerial characteristics. Both tended to be confident and responsible, with take-charge personalities. In addition, the female students ranked high in so-called masculine characteristics, such as tough-mindedness and suspiciousness. Meanwhile, the males scored high in the stereotyped feminine characteristics of humility,

THE STEREOTYPING PROBLEM

People who believe stereotypes tend to think their beliefs are fact based, making the beliefs hard to change. Research shows men and women in organizations are more alike than different. Yet a study revealed that both genders subscribe to stereotypes. The employees attributed caretaking qualities to women and leadership skills to men. However, each saw his or her own gender as excelling in problem-solving. Psychologists indicate that people tend to remember what confirms their own beliefs. However, as people come to know individuals that are different from themselves, they begin to let go of their stereotyped ideas.

tenderness, trust, and imagination. The researchers hypothesized that the women may have been mentally preparing themselves to work in settings with mostly men, while the men, being in the majority, felt they didn't have to prove themselves.

DO STEREOTYPES STILL HAVE AN IMPACT?

While it has not always been so, young women today are as likely as young men to want to climb to higher, more demanding sorts of positions, regardless of whether

A woman's leadership opportunities are impacted by her age, health, sexual orientation, and race.

they have children. What prospects greet this ambition? Some believe young women need not worry about gender discrimination. They cite statistics such as the income of young, single women living in the city, which is higher than that of similar men. They also point to well-known examples of women who hold prominent positions. Another factor that represents progress for women is that, while women were once excluded from higher education, their numbers now exceed those of men in colleges and universities. However, this optimistic view ignores the reversal that takes place later as women move up in their companies and have families.

Two Cornell University professors argued that the discrimination label is often no longer relevant. Few women work in science, technology, engineering and math (STEM) fields, and the professors believe that

BEHIND THE SILVER SCREEN

The film industry is filled with many talented female stars, and it's hard to imagine that sexism would be a problem. But Hollywood is under fire for its lack of women film and television directors. Directors significantly shape what the audience sees. They make decisions on who is hired, how roles are interpreted, and how the movie or show is filmed. In other words, they're the bosses. However, most directors are men, despite the fact that there are an even number of men and women at film schools. Once on the job, female directors report being questioned about their experiences and decision-making by crew members. A recent study of women in film in 2016 showed that the number of female directors in the top 250 films was just 7 percent, a drop from 2015's 9 percent.[3]

CHANGING MORE THAN GENDER

A Stanford University professor of neurobiology, Ben Barres, lived to see both sides of the gender divide. Ben was born female and was given the name Barbara. Like most professors, he was respected, but he gained more respect after undergoing a transition to alter his birth sex to male. A faculty member, thinking there were two Professor Barreses, commented that Barres gave a great seminar, adding "his work is much better than his sister's."[5]

continuing to cry discrimination distracts people from the real causes of the low numbers. Among these, they maintain, are the expectations women have developed involving family, lifestyle, and career choices.

There is certainly truth to this. Culture and upbringing shape people. Traditionally, girls and women have been led to think that STEM careers are not for them. This socialization process is one of the problems feminists have long critiqued. A striking example is a 1992 talking Barbie doll that announced, "Math class is tough!"[4] The doll was soon recalled following protests. Psychologists call the tendency people have to live out what is expected of them a self-fulfilling prophecy.

SELF-FULFILLING PROPHECY

Self-fulfilling prophecies may easily appear in the workplace. If a job requires little skill and has a low wage with no clear path to advancement, workers have little motivation to improve skills. The worker fulfills what the employer expects, which is not much. At the same time, the employer's feelings about that worker's capacity are confirmed as he or she sees little or no effort to improve.

This fulfilling of expectations may also be at work in the form of what some call a stereotype threat. Researchers noticed that women performed worse in mixed-gender groups when told they had a tough task involving what is considered a weak area for women. For example, when people are present who might judge them and they are told they have a difficult math assignment, the women tended to do poorly. Yet a group composed only of women who were not warned of the task's difficulty handled the same task and noted that it was not difficult. The experiment showed that expectations and judgment play a role in performance.

DISCUSSION STARTERS

- What other nursery rhymes, old sayings, and children's stories can you think of that suggest what it means to be male or female? What effects do such messages have on children?

- How do gender stereotypes shape men's career choices? Has the attention paid to these stereotypes opened up new opportunities to men?

- What advantages and disadvantages might there be to a mixed-gender team in the workplace?

CHAPTER FOUR

THE CHANGING FACE OF SEXUAL HARASSMENT

FOX:
RE SEXUAL PREDATOR
BILL O'REILLY

ultra ⓞ violet

When Diane Williams went to work as a public information specialist for the US Justice Department, she soon became aware of the romances married supervisors were engaging in with single female employees. Even more disturbing, she noticed a clear connection: women involved with a boss were promoted and got the best work assignments. Unwilling to be swept into such a situation, Williams turned down her boss's repeated requests for an affair. A few months later, she was fired.

Williams's case, which was settled in court in 1976, was the first to succeed with a claim of quid pro quo, meaning "this for that." In other words, someone in a position of authority makes promises to an employee in return for sexual favors. Quid pro quo had been a common practice in the 1970s and before. And when offenders were taken to court prior to Williams's case, judges had taken the position that sexual

HE SAID/SHE SAID CASES

Most sexual harassment complaints fail to develop into EEOC or state agencies' cases. Without written evidence of a raise-for-sex situation or sexually abusive language, the situations can be tough to prove. They turn into cases of he said/she said. Employers may cite poor performance or other reasons for demotions or firings. A onetime inappropriate joke won't pass the standard for a sexual harassment claim. Employees have stronger cases when they support claims with witnesses and dated records of repeated problems.

attraction and favors might occur in any mixed-gender work environment.

Bosses hold the job security and economic welfare of their employees in their hands. Employees might feel forced to give in to quid pro quo demands when they depend on the income from that job. With the laws against quid pro quo in place, instances have become less frequent and subtler.

WHEN THE WORKPLACE IS HOSTILE

A second kind of sexual harassment is creating a hostile work environment. Like quid pro quo, it is described under Title VII of the Civil Rights Act. As the Supreme Court notes, this law ensures employees' "right to work in an environment free from discriminatory intimidation, ridicule, and insult whether based on sex, race, religion, or national origin."[1] A hostile work environment is a far more common complaint than quid quo pro. Generally, the target must demonstrate that there is

CHALLENGES IN THE MILITARY

Although women have served in the military for generations, even in combat situations since 2015, they have continued to face discriminatory treatment, harassment, and even assault. In 2005, the Department of Defense responded by creating a Sexual Assault Prevention and Response Office. Despite progress, its 2015 annual report confirms hundreds of valid sexual harassment complaints are still made.

a collection of problems or repeated instances to prove his or her case. Such abuse takes place in various work settings, but it is naturally most common in jobs with a strong masculine culture.

In one Massachusetts case, a female finance officer in a car dealership was sexually harassed by her supervisor. He made inappropriate comments about female anatomy, tossed coins at her chest, and grabbed her. The jury agreed that she had been subjected to a hostile work environment because of her gender, directing that the company pay her $540,000.[2] Examples of situations creating hostile working environments are varied, ranging from the posting of lewd pictures to inappropriate jokes, comments, questions, suggestions, and touching.

Derogatory comments are a form of sexual harassment.

MICROAGGRESSIONS

"Though overt sexism against women within organizations may be starting to decline, many scholars fear that discrimination is not disappearing but rather has become more subtle," say Tessa Basford, Lynn Offermann, and Tara Behrend in the study "Do You See What I See? Perceptions of Gender Microaggressions in the Workplace."[3]

As is clear from their article title, they are concerned with actions referred to as microaggressions. They define the term as "intentional or unintentional actions or behaviors that exclude, demean, insult, oppress, or otherwise express hostility or indifference toward women."[4] Microaggressions encompass clear acts of abuse, discrimination, and prejudice. Microaggressions can also include demeaning words, tone, gestures, expressions, and jokes, as well as ignoring a person. They are subtle because they can be overlooked, even by those who commit them, and ambiguous because they can often be interpreted in more than one way, making the target unsure how to respond. In the case of a joke or teasing, microaggressions may even seem friendly on the surface. But such communications hurt the victim.

Microaggressions can frequently be seen in the workplace. In a hypothetical example provided by Basford,

Offermann, and Behrend, a senior research associate named Jennifer puts forth some ideas during a team meeting. The discussion rolls on and then Peter presents Jennifer's suggestions again—as if they are his. The boss praises Peter's contribution and requests that he put it in writing to be passed along. In another hypothetical example, Jessica, a finance associate, informs her boss about the successful presentation she planned and made to several possible customers. The boss responds, "So, who helped you with your presentation?" Both of these situations include microaggressions.

Interrupting can be another microaggression. Interruptions are common in conversations, but studies show that it is routine for men to interrupt women, no matter the setting. "Interruptions are attempts at dominance," explain Tonja Jacobi and Dylan Schweers in a *Harvard Business Review* article.[5] It would make sense, then, that as women rise in leadership, the interruptions would decrease. But even in the Supreme Court, female justices are frequently interrupted. Although women represent less than one quarter of the court's makeup, they are subject to nearly one-third of the interruptions. This number has increased along with the court's female membership. Conversely, only 4 percent of interruptions in the court were committed by female justices.[6]

During the 2016 presidential debates, Donald Trump frequently interrupted Hillary Clinton.

WHAT'S BEHIND THE HARASSMENT?

People hold stereotypes when a person has limited experience with the group being stereotyped. People are taught their judgments of other people from family, friends, and the larger culture. And, not having a clear reason to disagree, they accept the stereotypes uncritically. They may even accept stereotypes about themselves. For example, a man might buy into stereotypes about what it means to be a man or how a real man acts or thinks. It's when those ideas turn into actions that they cause problems in the workplace and elsewhere.

Social psychologist Jennifer Berdahl conducted a study that revealed that women who possessed traditionally masculine characteristics were harassed more often. Harassment against women also occurred more often in work situations predominantly involving male employees.

Berdahl concluded that "sexual harassment is driven not out of desire for women who meet feminine ideals, but out of a desire to punish those who violate them."[7] In other words, she feels it's a tool some men use to keep women in line with stereotypes. At the same time, it tends to make men feel more secure in their superior position.

WHOSE DOUBLE STANDARD?

When women are harassed for wearing what some consider provocative clothing, such as tight, short dresses, some men may shift the blame to women. Students of Katherine Gibbs School, formerly a popular secretarial school, once learned to present themselves as "pretty packages," though not necessarily provocative ones. But extending the idea, one writer asked: why wouldn't men think they were meant to unwrap the package?

Though most female workers reject the idea, some women did and do use their looks and flirtatiousness to get ahead. When this occurs, it's not uncommon for men to suggest that women are playing on men's weaknesses and cry double standard. They note if women can use their sexuality, why should men be vulnerable to harassment charges for responding to an apparent invitation? Supporters of sexual harassment legislation point out, though, that sexual harassment looks quite different than an invitation.

DISCUSSION STARTERS

- What are some of the various ways a person could handle a quid pro quo situation? What are the advantages and disadvantages of each?
- Microaggressions are subtle and can be confusing. How can the examples of microaggressions given here be interpreted differently?
- Should female employees expect to be treated differently based on how they dress? How might differences of opinion and culture affect how they are viewed? Is the standard different for men?

CHAPTER FIVE

SEXUAL HARASSMENT DOES DAMAGE

Filing a sexual harassment claim doesn't necessarily mean the harassment will stop.

positions is an example of the cost of special treatment. Because of this, women miss the opportunities to stretch and grow in their careers and to demonstrate new competencies that might lead to promotions.

TIME TO QUIT?

Studies suggest up to 80 percent of women quit jobs because of bullying, with sexual harassment being one form of that.[6] But there are more consequences to quitting than the upheaval of finding and adapting to a new workplace, which may be difficult. If workers leave a company after only a short time, or develop a pattern of quitting, employers may be reluctant to hire them, fearing they won't be committed to the organization or wondering if they were forced to quit and are likely to cause trouble. It's often difficult to step into a new job at the same pay rate the employee had previously. The new employee may have to start at the bottom and work her way up again. And because women collectively have a higher quit rate than men, individual women are judged as part of the whole. This makes the prospect of getting a new job more difficult. In short, quitting often damages workers' careers.

Perhaps these reasons, along with economic necessity, are why many women tend to stay with jobs even in the face of harassment. Quitting might also be seen as allowing the harassers to win. In some situations, remaining might be too much to expect of a harassed employee. But a toxic work culture might be more susceptible to shifts if women stay, work their way up the ladder, and create change themselves.

DISCUSSION STARTERS

- What similarities do you imagine there might be in people's responses to battlefield trauma and to sexual harassment?
- Brainstorm some effective responses to unwanted help or advice. How can these responses be done without damaging relationships?
- How can a climate be created that doesn't tolerate sexual harassment?

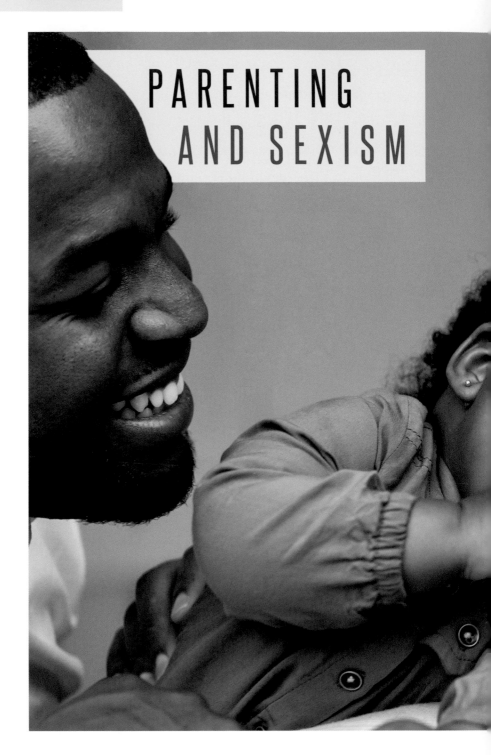

CHAPTER SIX

PARENTING
AND SEXISM

More than half of Americans support paid leave for fathers. But fathers who ask for it often endure workplace penalties such as poor recommendations and few rewards. Childcare was once seen almost entirely as the mother's responsibility. But today's fathers dedicate more time to raising children, and just as many fathers as mothers wish they could stay home with their children. The majority of the most economically sound countries in the world, aside from the United States, offer paid leave to fathers as well as mothers.

PARENTAL LEAVE FOR DADS

The majority of US fathers take parental leave for a new family member. A Department of Labor report indicates several benefits from fathers' presence during those early days. Both mothers and fathers need time to bond with their newborns. Babies and toddlers who experience greater father involvement gain in intelligence, good behavior, and mental health. Paternal leave also allows fathers to share childcare and household chores with the mother and handle the demands of work and home more successfully, and it enables mothers to return to work sooner, often on a full-time basis, contributing to the family income.

Most American families with children under 18 have two wage earners contributing to family finances. In some families, both parents work to provide a higher standard of living or because they enjoy working. Others scramble to make ends meet and may barely do that despite the dual incomes. In the country's 11 million single-parent homes the parent can rarely choose not to work.[4] Without paid

The small amount of time off parents receive after having children can cause stress in households.

leave, many pregnant women work nearly to the end of the pregnancy and resume employment soon after the birth because they can't afford not to. However, in addition to providing the mothers time to recuperate, studies show that paid leave is linked to preventing infant death and increasing the child's intelligence and resistance to disease.

Approximately 36 percent of women stay at home full-time with their children.

leave the workforce for an extended period don't succeed in finding new jobs. Others return to work part-time. Even if they return to full-time work, it may not be in an equivalent position or at equal pay. One study shows women's annual incomes are cut by nearly one-third following only one year's absence.[7]

In addition to whatever guilt and sense of loss mothers may feel at their decision to continue working, they often experience pressure from society to stay home with the children, even though women make up nearly half of the workforce. Pressure often comes from family as well. "We receive so many mixed messages about what we're supposed to want, what we're supposed to be," comments Deborah Graham, mother of three.[8]

A Harvard study supports the choice made by working mothers and suggests that daughters of mothers who work outside of the home will eventually climb to higher paid, more responsible careers than those of stay-at-home mothers. Meanwhile, their sons will learn to help with chores and childcare.

DISCUSSION STARTERS

- Do you believe parental benefits such as paid leave and childcare should be made available by the government, be required of employers, or left as they currently are? Explain your reasoning.
- Should American fathers be guaranteed parental leave? Why or why not?
- What are the benefits for children who have a parent at home with them? What are the benefits for children whose parents work full-time?

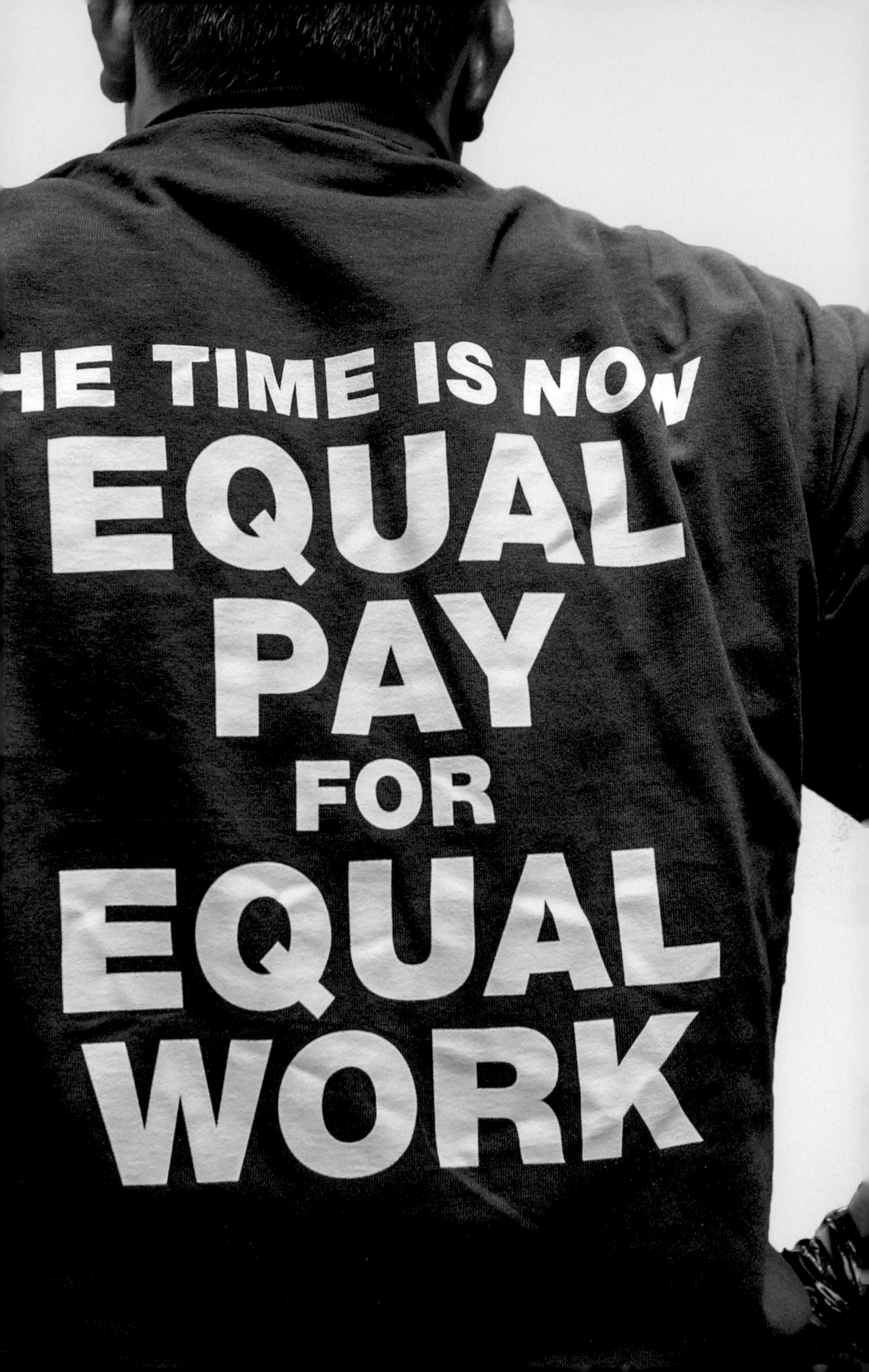
HE TIME IS NOW
EQUAL
PAY
FOR
EQUAL
WORK

UNEQUAL PAY FOR EQUAL WORK

By December 2016, television star Oprah Winfrey's earnings stacked up to billions of dollars. That there were two ahead of her on *Forbes* magazine's list of the wealthiest celebrities probably didn't bother her. Nor was Sheryl Sandberg, Facebook's chief operating officer, likely upset to find herself at number 12 on the *Forbes* 2017 list of "America's Richest Self-Made Women."

But Winfrey and Sandberg's situations are rarities. Most women experience a significant wage gap in comparison with men. For every dollar a male dentist, computer programmer, or chef makes, female workers in each field make 72 cents.[1]

Most full-time female workers in the United States earned an hourly wage in 2015, rather than a guaranteed annual income, such as a salary. Someone earning an hourly wage—usually in a lower-income position—receives income based on each hour worked. High-income positions are usually paid for doing the job, no matter how long it takes. A worker, for example, might earn $50,000 per year. She might work more than 40 hours per week, but that does not increase her income. Most hourly income jobs pay close to minimum wage. The median, or midpoint in the range, of female earnings is $12.56 per hour compared with $14.67 for men.[2] This equates to approximately $26,000 annually for women, placing them close to the 2017 federal poverty level for a family of four: $24,600.[3]

UNEVEN PROGRESS

Looking back to 1963, women made 59 percent of what men made.[4] However, the pursuit of equality may not be responsible for the increase in women's pay. During that time, men's salaries declined, perhaps due in part to new technological demands, narrowing the gap between genders. As it became less possible for men to support families without assistance, more women became permanently installed in the workplace and the family's financial structure.

Then progress ground to a near halt. From 2004 to 2015, women's pay has stagnated between 80 and 83 percent of men's.[5] This is despite the fact that women with college

THE HIGH COST OF WORKING

Beyond childcare is a host of other work-related expenses that may not be obvious, such as transportation, clothing, and equipment. The costs of many goods and services hit women harder than men, and not only because women earn less. Women's products cost 7 percent more on average than men's.[6] For example, the average cost for men's dress pants is $71.71. The average women's dress pants cost $75.66.[7] Dry cleaning of a man's shirt costs on average $2.06, whereas for a woman's blouse the cost is $3.95. According to a California study, this so-called pink tax costs women an extra $1,351 annually.[8]

degrees outnumber their male counterparts by a small margin. When women move up the ladder to more powerful positions, their incomes drop to 79 cents for each dollar earned by a man in a comparable position.[9]

WHY EQUAL PAY ISN'T STANDARD

Equal pay for equal work has long been a rallying cry for women and those who advocate for fairness. It's easy to chalk the problem up to discrimination against women, but the reasons for unequal pay are more complicated. For example, women with children generally earn less than women without. However, men used to receive a raise, known as the "family wage," when a child arrived, contributing to the gap in pay between women and men. Stemming from the idea that men had sole responsibility of providing for the family, the now-illegal family wage is still quietly given to new fathers by some bosses.

Parenting is tied to other causes of the pay gap as well. With children often comes the need for shorter or more flexible work hours and time away from the job. The flexibility advantage costs women financially and often forces them out of their chosen fields and into less profitable ones.

Another edge many men and women without children have is the ability to work extra hours. "In business and finance, workers are richly compensated for pulling marathon workweeks, and the pay gap looks like a canyon," points out Jordan Weissmann, author of *The Pay Gap Prescription*.[10] Women leave college with their graduate degrees in business, and land jobs with about the same salaries as male graduates. However, once children begin to arrive, their salaries plummet. In a long-term study of business school graduates, for example, economist Claudia Goldin and colleagues found that with motherhood came a salary drop of 45 percent.[11]

Flexibility isn't the only reason women veer toward low-paying professions. Girls are sometimes socialized

More men than women have the opportunity to work overtime for increased pay.

In recent years, there has been a push by educational institutes to encourage girls to get involved in STEM fields.

to lean toward roles traditionally associated with women, such as teaching, nursing, and secretarial positions. Playing with dolls and other family and household-oriented toys, playing school, and being mother's helpers are all encouraged. All of this is reinforced by messages outside the home, if not inside it. These positions were once among the only roles open to women. They became ingrained in the national consciousness as natural fits for women.

In the 1980s through the 1990s, many women headed for nontraditional roles to become firefighters, engineers, and computer programmers. Recent attention encourages girls to look toward careers in STEM. However, the rush toward the nontraditional jobs has declined, perhaps because the number of women in the workforce overall is decreasing. In the 1990s, the United States was a world leader in its number of working women. In 2017, percentages for working women aged 25 through 54 dropped from 74 percent in 1999 to 69 percent, and many women cite unsupportive work policies for families as the reason.[12] And only 5 percent of women work in STEM and other male-dominated fields.[13]

ASK FOR WHAT THEY WANT

Some suggest that women don't get higher salaries simply because they don't ask for them. More than one-half of men negotiate when they discuss job offers. They tell the boss why they deserve more. Many employers expect negotiation, and men who do are often given

THE STATE OF THE PAY GAP

Although the average pay gap between genders is approximately 20 percent, it changes significantly throughout the country. For example, in New York and Delaware, women earn on average 89 percent of men's earnings, followed by Florida at 87 percent. At the low end are North Dakota, Utah, and West Virginia at 71 percent. In last place are Louisiana at 68 percent and Wyoming at 64 percent.[14]

HOW WOMEN CAN ASK FOR MORE

Mika Brzezinski, author of *Knowing Your Value,* advises women to search and plan so they know of other opportunities available to them before negotiating their pay. Being unafraid to decline a job or quit puts them in the best bargaining position when a company wants them. Women should brainstorm why they deserve raises by looking at their experience, qualifications, and accomplishments.

Business adviser and television personality Suze Orman suggests that when they meet with the boss, women should try to open a conversation rather than ask yes or no questions that can easily be dismissed. Orman also advises offering high and low figures for the proposed salary, the low being the one they think they can get.

higher salaries. The majority of women do not try negotiating.

Why? Part of it may be socialization. American society tells women they are not supposed to make waves or seem greedy, nor are they supposed to brag about their achievements. Studies have shown when women argue for higher pay or better benefits, they are less likely to be hired, whether the interviewer is a man or a woman.

BLEAKER PICTURE FOR WOMEN OF COLOR

Most women of color deal not only with gender discrimination but also prejudice against their race and ethnicity. This translates into hourly wages or salaries that are lower than those of white women. While white women have established themselves in legal and medical fields, for example, only 3 to 4 percent of women of color are represented in those professions.[15] The picture is similar for women of color as corporate leaders and in the STEM fields.

Asian-American women fare better than others in this group, coming closest to pay equal to white men's earnings. For African-American and Hispanic women, that median hourly wage drops to $11.39 hourly (compared to white men's $14.93) or approximately $23,700 annually, which is below the federal poverty level.[16]

Pay gaps vary from state to state, as does how women of color are treated in the workplace. But bearing that variation in mind, the findings of the National Women's Law Center are profound. It reports that, with the pay gap remaining as it is today, white, non-Hispanic women working 40 years stand to lose $565,640 because of the pay gap.[17] For black women, the loss is more than doubled, at $840,040; Hispanic women edge near $1,043,800; Native

THE COLOR OF WAGE DIFFERENCE

Although women earn less than men, the numbers break down further by race. Compared with white, non-Hispanic men, Asian women earn the highest, at 90 cents for every $1 of men's earnings. White women come next at approximately 76 cents, followed by African-American women at 62 cents, Native Hawaiians and other Pacific Islanders at 60 cents, and Native Americans and Native Alaskans at 58 cents. Hispanic or Latina women are last, earning only 54 cents for white, non-Hispanic men's $1.[18] Although the gap varies, it affects almost every job category.

American women slip in between the two at $943,240;
Asian-American women sustain a significant lifetime loss
at $349,320.[19]

STRIKING OUT ON THEIR OWN

With all these pitfalls on the road to fair pay, many
women think of starting their own businesses and

Businesses owned by women and with a focus on traditionally female areas
tend to earn less money than men's businesses.

becoming entrepreneurs. Entrepreneurs, after all, tend to earn more and as bosses, they can make their own rules and schedules. Women-owned businesses have increased by 30 percent since 2007 to roughly 36 percent of the 27.6 million US businesses.[20] Many of these businesses focus on the traditionally female areas of health care, human services, and education.

One problem these businesses face is getting funding. Investors tend to fund those with whom they have some connection. When women do get the start-up money, the loan company generally charges them much higher interest rates and requires more collateral to guarantee loan repayment in case the business fails. Lenders view women's businesses as risky investments. The owners often have less of their own money to commit, and the businesses tend to be smaller.

DISCUSSION STARTERS

- Why do you think there is a difference in pay between women based on their race?
- Why do you think women who ask for a higher salary may be viewed as greedy? Do you believe men face the same response? Why or why not?
- How should the value of a job be determined?

CHAPTER EIGHT

THE GLASS CEILING

Sheryl Sandberg knew how to fully commit herself academically and in the workplace. She graduated as Harvard University's star student in economics and started her career as chief of staff for the US treasury secretary. In 2001, she took a chance and became the general manager of business for Google, which was then a new and struggling business. The company soon took off, and Sandberg became a vice president. Then, Facebook founder Mark Zuckerberg persuaded her to become his company's chief operating officer. A friend who encouraged Sandberg to take the Google job told her the company was "a rocket ship," ready to blast off.[1] So too, it seems, was Sandberg.

That isn't the story for many female would-be leaders. Most haven't been able to breach the glass ceiling, which is a metaphor for the invisible barricade against women rising to leadership positions. The lack of female representation is especially apparent in government. It puts the United States behind much of the world. For example, ranked with 49 high-income nations, the United States is thirty-third in having women in important governmental positions.[2] In Fortune 500 companies, which are the most profitable businesses in the United States, the portion of female CEOs has risen from

Although the trend for female leadership is upward, women are still minorities in these roles.

zero percent in 1995 to slightly more than 5 percent in early 2017.[3] Women on the boards of those companies numbered 20.2 percent.[4]

Research suggests it's the motherhood penalty at work, but some Americans surveyed by the Pew Research Center said the problem is the double standard. Women have to outshine men to rise to the top. Others suggest neither voters nor corporations can accept female leaders yet. Despite this, those surveyed see women being better at compromising and as more honest than men. In addition, women are seen as more consistent in assigning workers'

PROFESSIONS BY THE NUMBERS IN 2016[7]

AIRCRAFT PILOT AND FLIGHT ENGINEERS
WOMEN: 5.9%
MEN: 94.1%

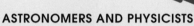
ASTRONOMERS AND PHYSICISTS
WOMEN: 20%
MEN: 80%

COMPUTER PROGRAMMERS
WOMEN: 25.7%
MEN: 74.3%

DOCTORS AND SURGEONS
WOMEN: 38%
MEN: 62%

LAWYERS
WOMEN: 40%
MEN: 60%

pay and benefits fairly and in mentoring young workers, while men are believed more able to take risks and argue for the best deals.

However, Barbara Roberts, business expert and originator of the term *glass ceiling,* suggests that the majority of baby boomer women simply weren't interested in business leadership. "If you look at the percentage of women at the top today," she comments, "it's really not that bad in context."[5] With the higher number of millennial women interested in leadership, the future looks more promising for women in business.

LEADERSHIP WITH A WOMAN'S TOUCH

Similar to many female business leaders, Sandberg recognized that the amount of women in positions of power in corporate America was extremely small, and she wanted to encourage more women into the ranks. Women keep themselves below the ceiling, she felt, because of uncertainties about wielding power, family concerns, and lack of support at home. Instead of leaning away from these situations, Sandberg wants them to go after opportunities wholeheartedly, as successful men have. "If more women lean in," she argues, "we can change the power structure of our world and expand opportunities for all."[6] Some call this goal too optimistic, arguing that

Female leaders can use their distinct skills to help a company succeed.

history doesn't support the idea. In addition, they argue, there are too many women with insufficient education or who are caught in jobs that don't offer advancement.

With limited numbers of women in top positions, some women feel they need to adopt male leadership styles of competition and aggression to succeed. "Be yourself," advises Hilary Genga, the founder of a swimwear company. "Don't conform yourself to a man's idea of what a leader should look like."[8] When they act like themselves, women often find they contribute unique abilities to the company. Researchers identified actions leaders use to help their companies succeed. They found five that women exhibited more frequently than men: inspiring, having high expectations, rewarding achievement, helping employees develop, and acting as role models.

Female leaders bring other advantages to their companies as well, including greater diversity throughout the organization. Sandberg argues, "Endless data show that diverse teams make better decisions. We are building products that people with very diverse backgrounds use, and I think we all want our company makeup to reflect the makeup of the people who use our products."[9]

PERCHED ON THE GLASS CLIFF

At the same time, women and minorities often find that they've broken through the glass ceiling only to discover themselves perched on a glass cliff. In other words, they are put in a high, but precarious, position where the ground may give way beneath them. This more recent metaphor embraces businesses as being in crisis (the glass cliff), and it's during crisis periods that women and minorities are often hired to improve a company's image and financial health.

This was the case for Marissa Mayer, hired as CEO in 2012 to bring Yahoo out of a slump when she was only 37. Mayer arrived with an impressive resume. As an engineer and computer programmer, she spent more than ten years with Google, helping it become the major Internet company it is today. Mayer used all her strategies, including ideas that had worked well at Google, but nothing seemed to turn the company around. In 2017, after Yahoo's sale to Verizon, the company began planning her departure.

Mayer is one example of the glass cliff problem. From the perspective of the companies' leaders, they may feel they should try something radically different, such as a woman or minority CEO, to see if that will push the company past its difficulty. In the end, insists Professor Elizabeth Dickinson of the University of North Carolina, "If you do well [people think], it's because of your gender. If you don't do well, it's because of your gender."[10]

A study of this new predicament showed that women often sought out these crisis positions. Many reason that, considering the difficulty of getting into leadership, women have to highlight their abilities. And what is more effective than turning around a company in trouble? In the process of working for these companies, women build a specialty, a strong set of skills, and a reputation for crisis management.

However, even when hired to save a struggling company, women aren't always given sufficient support and tools to do so. Sometimes they are barred from crucial decision-making necessary to enact their strategies. Lack of support among coworkers, as well as those above and even below them, can further hamper their efforts. Additional factors include extreme pressure to succeed and judgements on not only their performance but also their personal style, including appearance. These elements make for an unhealthy work environment. Researchers Christy Glass and Alison Cook of Utah State University point out, "Women with authority in the workplace exhibit significantly more symptoms of depression than men with authority or women without authority."[11] Under such difficult circumstances, some female leaders complete the task they were hired for and retire or find another line of work. They are also fired or asked to leave more often than are male CEOs.

DISCUSSION STARTERS

- Why do you suppose the United States has fewer female leaders than some other countries?
- Do you think female and male business leaders have different strengths to bring to companies? Support your answer.
- Would the prospect of a hostile work environment discourage you from considering a job? What would be the advantages of pursuing the job?

TODAY'S
TRAILBLAZERS

URSULA BURNS: CEO OF XEROX

Ursula Burns grew up in a poor Manhattan, New York, neighborhood. Determined not to let race, poverty, or gender block her, Burns grabbed opportunities and got a solid education. She became the first African-American woman to lead a major firm when she was named CEO of the Xerox Corporation, a company providing document-copying services and equipment.

RUTH BADER GINSBURG: SUPREME COURT JUSTICE

As a Harvard law student in the 1950s, Ruth Bader Ginsburg was scolded for seeking to take jobs from men. But President Bill Clinton appointed her to the Supreme Court in 1993, the second of just four women justices as of 2017.

WINONA LaDUKE: ENVIRONMENTALIST, ACTIVIST AND WRITER

Harvard- and Antioch-educated Winona LaDuke, a member of the Ojibwe tribe, has a dizzying array of accomplishments and awards. As the program director of Honor the Earth, she addresses environmental, peace, equality, and justice issues in the United States and internationally. She was also a candidate for vice president in 1996 and 2000 with the Green Party's nominee, Ralph Nader.

ELLEN OCHOA: ASTRONAUT AND INVENTOR

As Ellen Ochoa grew up in the late 1950s and 1960s, no female astronauts existed. She never imagined she would become the first Latina astronaut in 1991 and spend hundreds of hours in space. Now she is a spacecraft communicator in mission control.

CHAPTER NINE

WHAT'S NEXT FOR WOMEN AT WORK?

"Women's subordination is an ancient human practice," write the authors of *Feminism Unfinished*.[1] Women's roles have been deeply embedded into American society through social, economic, cultural, and political practices. The authors note it will take generations to overcome gender inequalities. They take a balanced view of the situation today, though, commenting, "While women have made tremendous gains since the 1960s, we still live in a 'half-changed world.'"[2]

With the help of technology, feminists of contemporary America have a more global perspective, sharing issues and news across the world. With continuing problems such as lack of paid parental leave, insufficient numbers of female elected leadership, and persistent traditional notions about gender affecting the culture, the United States has lost its place as a leader in women's rights. Its problems are also not considered to be as urgent as those in countries where girls and women are struggling for basic rights like education. Today's feminists haven't gathered around a single issue as the feminists did before, though. Some people believe not having a narrow aim on which to focus its energies robs feminism of power, while others believe it indicates how widely feminism has spread throughout modern culture.

However, three general ideas do seem to characterize today's feminists. The movement continues to embrace diverse viewpoints and backgrounds, and it remains multicultural. It also views feminism as one of many interconnected social justice efforts. In addition, it recognizes feminism can't be pinned down to a single approach and that expressing feminist ideas can be as complex and diverse as women themselves.

COUNTERACTING STEREOTYPING

Correcting workplace sexism requires diverse approaches. One approach has focused on correcting subtle gender bias in choosing leaders and valuing a person's work. Such an approach has proved successful within

LOOKING UP AND DOWN THE JOB LADDER

While more women move up the corporate ladder and into positions that had been previously unavailable to them, more work is created for those at the lower end, who are often women. Career women with working husbands sometimes need helpers, such as housekeepers, childcare workers, and others, to relieve them of household tasks. The rights and needs of these women, overwhelmingly immigrants and women of color, also need to be considered.

Ai-Jen Poo, the daughter of immigrant parents, founded the National Domestic Workers Alliance in 2010. At one time, these workers had few rights. Often living in the homes where they worked, they might have been required to work at any time day or night, deprived of days off, and underpaid. Over the years, laws have secured rights for these workers. Poo's organization continues that work, uniting workers across the country and the world and winning them respect and political power.

Hiring applicants based on their qualifications and not their gender can help women obtain more leadership roles.

the historically male-dominated departments of medicine, science, and engineering at University of Wisconsin–Madison.

Rather than blame faculty for stereotyping, these researchers recognized that the behavior was often an unconscious mind-set and habit and not a deliberate attempt to give men higher status. They set out to educate faculty in a two-and-a-half-hour workshop. They began by making them aware of gender bias in their fields and then appealing to the faculty's goals of advancing those fields. They educated faculty about the history of stereotyping, how it appears today, and how it works against their goals.

Finally, they gave faculty five methods to help them change their thinking and behavior. Now that faculty could recognize their own stereotypic thinking, they were encouraged to replace such thoughts with more accurate impressions when they occurred. They were also asked to learn more about those they dealt with in order to see them as individuals, and to look for meaningful ways to connect with exceptions to the stereotypes, such as successful female scientists or leaders. The remaining two strategies drew on participants' imaginations: imagining the feelings of a person who is stereotyped and, when hiring, imagining a woman successfully handling the job. Several months after this workshop, participants continued to show positive changes in thinking and behavior.

RAISING A NEW GENERATION OF STEREOTYPE BREAKERS

When racial integration was enforced in schools and housing in the mid-1900s, people came face-to-face with those from different backgrounds. As people learned more about each other, stereotypes began to break down and knowledge began to replace ignorance. It was all about exposure. Though racial problems persist, and much still needs to be accomplished, more people came to see each other as individuals, rather than generalized members of a group. It created a sea change in society's attitudes and opened up new opportunities.

After people recognize their prejudices they can work to combat them.

Exposure to girls and women who defy stereotypes produces the same results. This is one reason why encouraging girls to explore nontraditional roles, such as leadership positions and STEM jobs, is important. Many organizations and educators have taken up this cause. It is vital for girls and boys to see females in nontraditional roles. Gender identity forms early, so it is important to begin counteracting stereotypes early.

Organizations can do their part by letting job applicants know what credentials are needed, by helping employees root out their own prejudices and those built into their organizations, and by judging all workers by the same standards. Years ago, for example, orchestras were largely male. Then they began conducting blind auditions in which judges could not see the person playing. With this practice, the number of women hired doubled. This practice can be used during the hiring process at businesses as well. Diversity in the workplace includes gender, and this diversity should be supported with a diversity committee or staff and with training programs.

Diversity training and increased education on the nature and origin of gender bias is expected to decrease microaggressions. But overt sexual harassment requires overt action. Organizations can send a clear message by enforcing their sexual harassment policies and by offering counseling. When they do, those targeted feel taken seriously, valued, and supported. They then feel more committed to the organization. Such a response also reduces sexual harassment incidents.

THE FIGHT FOR FAMILIES

Families are a basic unit of any society. Viewing society as an interlaced set of systems helps reveal how a failing family affects the whole. For example, a mother returning to work too soon after giving birth might become ill and end up in the hospital, forcing her to be absent from work without any plans made to accommodate it. If unsupervised, a troubled child steals from a store, and the store loses income. Police and lawyers might become involved, increasing the burden in the court system. When women struggle alone to balance work and family, negative effects spread beyond themselves to impact others. Each member within a family must have his or her rights valued and supported.

MomsRising, which emerged in 2006, is an example of a group "united by the goal of building a more family-friendly America."[3] Early on, it created a "Motherhood Manifesto" insisting on paid parental leave; flexible working hours and places of work; good educational, after-school facilities; reasonably priced, quality childcare; a livable minimum wage; pay equal to men's for equivalent work; and an end to the motherhood penalty. In short, the group identified nearly every obstacle for mothers in the workplace and worked to remedy it.

Today, it has expanded its efforts to include such diverse issues as a clean environment, guaranteed health care, immigration fairness, and gun safety. Other groups such as

FLEXIBILITY RISING

Half of the women surveyed by the Working Mother Research Institute indicate that balancing family and work needs remains difficult. But increasing numbers of women find flexible scheduling and paid parental leave are becoming more common. Accountant Kelly Opferman is among those benefitting from her tax-services company adopting flexible scheduling. Rather than working a typical day from 8:30 a.m. to 5:30 p.m., Opferman lays out each day according to the work required, family needs, and her own plans. It's great for Opferman and works for the company as well. Although the company once had 22 percent of employees leaving, that number decreased to 8 percent.[4] The company is also making more money than ever.

NOW and Sistersong, geared to women of color, list reproductive justice—including the right to abortions and affordable birth control—among their efforts.

RESOLVING THE WAGE GAP

Although progress has been made to decrease the gender wage gap, researchers predict that true wage equality will not occur until 2059. Once the motherhood penalty is eliminated, and as stereotypes and barriers to nontraditional fields and leadership disappear, wages will rise.

In 2009, President Barack Obama signed the Lilly Ledbetter Fair Pay Act into law. Although President John F. Kennedy had signed the Equal Pay Act in 1963, it didn't help Lilly Ledbetter much. Ledbetter, a manager for the Goodyear Corporation, sued the company when she learned two men in similar positions made more than she did. The Supreme Court struck down the decision in her favor because more than 180 days had passed since the unequal wage had begun; Title VII of the Civil Rights Act of 1964 states that claims must be filed no more than 180 days after the initial offense. The act, named in Ledbetter's honor, eliminates the requirement to act quickly, as employees often don't know their coworkers' salaries.

When employers publish salary ranges for the positions they advertise, it helps prevent wage discrimination. In the past, employees couldn't legally ask about or discuss each other's salaries. Obama signed an executive order in 2014, leading to a Department of Labor rule eliminating that practice for those working for the federal government. This new transparency will help the country move toward equal pay, observes Catherine Hill, vice president for the American Association of University Women (AAUW).

A FINAL WORD

Beyond combating sexual harassment, discriminatory hiring, and unequal pay, many feel a deeper change is needed. Joan C. Williams and Rachel Dempsey, authors of *What Works for Women at Work,*

AFFIRMATIVE ACTION AND WOMEN

In recent years, many people have argued that affirmative action has outlived its use. The program, begun in 1961 by President Kennedy, helped people gain equal treatment in education and work "without regard to their race, creed, or national origin."[5] Six years later, President Lyndon B. Johnson added the word "sex" to the program. Still, it continues to be thought of as primarily protection against racial discrimination. Some argue that affirmative action is reverse discrimination, favoring minorities. Yet affirmative action has been a great advantage to women in education and work.

Studies show that white women make up the group most helped by the legislation and that in the private sector (where there is greater possibility of skirting the law without notice), "white women have moved in and up at numbers that far eclipse those of people of color," notes Jessie Daniels in an article for *Racism Review.*[6]

Positive outcomes occur when companies promote gender equality.

argue that "even if employers do everything else absolutely perfectly," they won't achieve equal numbers of working men and women "given that over 80 percent of women have children."[7] High-powered jobs often require 50-plus hours a week. Most women with children simply cannot commit that amount of time, nor can fathers who take primary care of their children.

Society can shrug and say the choice to be mothers counts women out, or it can decide it values the talent women offer. Companies can grant paid family leave to both parents and allow career breaks and reduced work hours for women and men "without falling off the career track," as Williams and Dempsey state.[8]

'Abdu'l-Bahá, an early 1900s leader of the Bahá'í Faith, wrote, "The world of humanity has two wings—one is women and the other men. Not until both wings are equally developed can the bird fly." Because of that, equal opportunity is essential. "Until womankind reaches the same degree as man, until she enjoys the same arena of activity, extraordinary attainment for humanity will not be realized."[9]

DISCUSSION STARTERS

- Can you think of additional ways, beyond feeling excluded from certain jobs, that stereotyping and sexism negatively affect men?
- What are some difficulties in securing equal pay for men and women in the same job positions?
- Would the sort of workshop held at the University of Wisconsin be helpful in your school or club?

ESSENTIAL FACTS

SIGNIFICANT EVENTS

- During World War I (1914–1918) and World War II (1939–1945), thousands of women stepped up to fill workplaces left empty by men who had gone to war. Once the wars were over, however, women were expected to return to homemaking.

- During the late 1960s and the 1970s, the women's liberation movement gathered momentum. Consciousness-raising groups helped women understand how they had been socialized to accept second-class citizenship.

- Several laws were passed to help ensure women are treated equally in education and in the workplace, among them Title VII of the Civil Rights Act (1964) and the Lilly Ledbetter Fair Pay Act (2009).

KEY PLAYERS

- Elizabeth Cady Stanton was an early suffragette who fought for women's rights, including an equal place in the working world.

- President John F. Kennedy's Commission on the Status of Women highlighted challenges that women in America faced. Although the commission's report excluded the concerns faced by women of color, it did pave the way for the establishment of the National Organization of Women.

- Although she lost her sexual harassment lawsuit against Supreme Court Justice Clarence Thomas, Anita Hill's case launched a national conversation on workplace harassment in the early 1990s.

IMPACT ON SOCIETY

Women had to win the right to vote and work in the United States. Over the years, opportunities have greatly increased, with women working in virtually every sector of society. But even though more than one-half of the women in the United States are now part of the labor force, discrimination and harassment continue to plague them. While laws intended to protect workers have paved the way to equality, the gender pay gap and other less-obvious forms of sexism persist.

QUOTE

"Be yourself. Don't conform yourself to a man's idea of what a leader should look like."

—Hilary Genga, the founder of a swimwear company

GLOSSARY

AMBIGUOUS
Having more than one possible meaning or interpretation.

CREDENTIALS
Qualifications.

DISPARAGING
Detracting from something, degrading.

EGALITARIAN
Believing in equal rights.

ENTREPRENEUR
A person who organizes and operates a business or businesses.

FEMINISM
The belief that women should have the same opportunities and rights as men politically, socially, and economically.

FOMENT
Agitate or stir up.

HYPOTHESIZE
To make an idea or explanation for something that is subject to scientific investigations.

LEWD

Suggestive or obscene.

MANDATE

To command.

OVERT

Easily seen.

SEX DISCRIMINATION

Discrimination in the workplace based on a person's sex.

SEXISM

Discrimination or prejudice toward people based on their sex.

SEXUAL HARASSMENT

Unwanted physical or verbal sexual advances.

SOCIALIZATION

Training or being prepared to fit into a group.

ADDITIONAL RESOURCES

SELECTED BIBLIOGRAPHY

Berebitsky, Julie. *Sex and the Office: A History of Gender, Power, and Desire*. New Haven, CT: Yale UP, 2012. Print.

Cobble, Dorothy Sue, Linda Gordon, and Astrid Henry. *Feminism Unfinished*. New York: Liveright, 2014. Print.

Williams, Joan C., and Rachel Dempsey. *What Works for Women at Work*. New York: New York UP, 2017. Print.

FURTHER READINGS

Higgins, Melissa, and Michael Regan. *The Gender Wage Gap*. Minneapolis, MN: Abdo, 2017. Print.

Reber, Deborah. *Doable: The Girls' Guide to Accomplishing Just About Anything*. New York: Simon, 2015. Print.

ONLINE RESOURCES

Booklinks
NONFICTION NETWORK
FREE! ONLINE NONFICTION RESOURCES

To learn more about sexism at work, visit **abdobooklinks.com**. These links are routinely monitored and updated to provide the most current information available.

MORE INFORMATION

For more information on this subject, contact or visit the following organizations:

GIRLS INC.
120 Wall Street
New York, NY 10005-3902
212-509-2000
girlsinc.org

Girls Inc. empowers and educates girls to break through barriers. The site includes news, opinion pieces, and chapters for girls to join around the country.

NATIONAL ORGANIZATION OF WOMEN
1100 H Street NW, Suite 300
Washington, DC 20005
202-628-8669
now.org

Learn about current issues and initiatives of the premier women's organization and how you can help.

NATIONAL WOMEN'S HISTORY PROJECT
730 Second Street #469, PO Box 469
Santa Rosa, CA 95402
707-636-2888
nwhp.org

The site offers information on women's history, including quizzes to test your knowledge.

SOURCE NOTES

CHAPTER 1. A PERSISTENT PROBLEM

1. Emily Keller. "One Case Against Wal-Mart." *Bloomberg*. Bloomberg L.P., 29 June 2007. Web. 14 Apr. 2017.

2. "Women's Economic Empowerment." *Walmart*. Wal-Mart Stores, n.d. Web. 1 Aug. 2017.

3. "Top WBENC Consumer Companies Join Together for the First Time in Collective Initiative to Source from Women-Owned Businesses." *Walmart*. Wal-Mart Stores, 29 Mar. 2017. Web. 1 Aug. 2017.

4. Emily Keller. "One Case Against Wal-Mart." *Bloomberg*. Bloomberg L.P., 29 June 2007. Web. 14 Apr. 2017.

5. Jordan Weissmann. "The Pay Gap Prescription." *Slate*. The State Group, 17 Mar. 2014. Web. 1 Aug. 2017.

6. Ibid.

7. "Pharmacy Solutions Pays $85,000 to Settle Pregnancy Discrimination Suit with EEOC." *U.S. Equal Employment Opportunity Commission*. U.S. Equal Employment Opportunity Commission, n.d. Web. 1 Aug. 2017.

8. Meghan Ross. "Fired Pharmacist Wins $31 Million from Walmart." *Pharmacy Times*. Pharmacy & Healthcare Communications, 1 Feb. 2016. Web. 1 Aug. 2017.

9. Jonathan Stempel. "Wal-Mart Owes Pharmacist $16.08 mln for Gender Bias, Sum May Drop." *CNBC*. CNBC, 10 Jan. 2017. Web. 12 June 2017.

10. "Charge Statistics (Charges Filed with EEOC) FY 1997 Through FY 2016." *U.S. Equal Employment Opportunity Commission.* U.S. Equal Employment Opportunity Commission, n.d. Web. 1 Aug. 2017.

CHAPTER 2. THE LONG STRUGGLE AGAINST SEXISM

1. "Letter from Abigail Adams to John Adams, 31 March–5 April 1776." *Massachusetts Historical Society*. Massachusetts Historical Society, n.d. Web. 1 Aug. 2017.

2. "Want Ads." *Teaching American History in South Carolina*. Teaching American History in South Carolina Project, n.d. Web. 1 Aug. 2017.

3. "African American Women in Defense of Ourselves." *Center for the Study of Political Graphics*. Center for the Study of Political Graphics, 2 Apr. 2014. Web. 1 Aug. 2017.

CHAPTER 3. IMPACT OF STEREOTYPES

1. James A. Schultz. *The Knowledge of Childhood in the German Middle Ages, 1100–1350*. Philadelphia, PA: U of Pennsylvania P, 1995. Print.

2. Dorothy Sue Cobble. *Feminism Unfinished*. New York: Liveright, 2014. Print.

3. Lisa Respers France. "Female Directors Becoming Rarer in Hollywood." *CNN*. Cable News Network, 12 Jan. 2017. Web. 13 June 2017.

4. "From Discouraged Math Student to Computer Engineer: One Doll's Story." *AAUW*. AAUW, 11 Dec. 2013. Web. 1 Aug. 2017.

5. Joan C. Williams and Rachel Dempsey. *What Works for Women at Work*. New York: New York UP, 2014. Print.

CHAPTER 4. THE CHANGING FACE OF SEXUAL HARASSMENT

1. "U.S. Equal Employment Opportunity Commission Enforcement Guidance." *U.S. Equal Employment Opportunity Commission*. U.S. Equal Employment Opportunity Commission, 19 Mar. 1990. Web. 1 Aug. 2017.

2. Kali Hays. "Mass. Court Restores $500K Against Co. Ignoring Harassment." *Law 360*. Portfolio Media, n.d. Web. 1 Aug. 2017.

3. Tessa E. Basford, Lynn R Offermann, and Tara S. Behrend, "Do You See What I See? Perceptions of Gender Microaggressions in the Workplace." *Psychology of Women Quarterly*. Society for the Psychology of Women, 19 Nov. 2013. Web. 1 Aug. 2017.

4. Ibid.

5. Tonja Jacobi and Dylan Schweers. "Female Supreme Court Justices Are Interrupted More by Male Justices and Advocates." *Harvard Business Review*. Harvard Business School, 11 Apr. 2017. Web. 1 Aug. 2017.

6. Ibid.

7. Joan C. Williams and Rachel Dempsey. *What Works for Women at Work*. New York: New York UP, 2014. Print.

CHAPTER 5. SEXUAL HARASSMENT DOES DAMAGE

1. Judith MacIntosh, Judith Wuest, Marilyn Ford-Gilboe, and Colleen Varcoe. "Cumulative Effects of Multiple Forms of Violence and Abuse on Women." *Violence and Victims*. 2015: 504. Print.

2. Barbara Kate Repa. "Job Consequences of Sexual Harassment." *NOLO*. Nolo, n.d. Web. 1 Aug. 2017.

3. Kaifeng Jiang, Ying Hong, Patrick F. McKay, Derek R. Avery, David C. Wilson, Sabrina D. Volpone. "Retaining Employees Through Anti-Sexual Harassment Practices: Exploring the Mediating Role of Psychological Distress and Employee Engagement." *Human Resources Management* 57.1 (2014): 2. Print.

4. Stefanie K Johnson, Jessica Kirk, and Ksenia Keplinger. "Why We Fail to Report Sexual Harassment. *Harvard Business Review*. Harvard Business School, 4 Oct. 2016. Web. 1 Aug. 2017.

5. Hannah Fingerhut. "In Both Parties, Men and Women Differ Over Whether Women Still Face Obstacles to Progress." *Pew Research Center*. Pew Research Center, 16 Aug. 2016. Web. 1 Aug. 2017.

6. Judith MacIntosh, Judith Wuest, Marilyn Ford-Gilboe, and Colleen Varcoe. "Cumulative Effects of Multiple Forms of Violence and Abuse on Women." *Violence and Victims* 30.3 (2015): 516. Print.

CHAPTER 6. PARENTING AND SEXISM

1. Rebecca Greenfield. "That Fantastic Parental Leave Policy Sweeping American? It Isn't." *Bloomberg*. Bloomberg, 13 Mar. 2017. Web. 1 Aug. 2017.

2. "Statistics on Stay-At-Home Dads." *National At-Home Dad Network*. National At-Home Dad Network, n.d. Web. 1 Aug. 2017.

3. Gretchen Livingston. "Growing Number of Dads at Home with the Kids." *Pew Research Center*. Pew Research Center, 5 June 2014. Web. 1 Aug. 2017.

4. "The Majority of Children Live with Two Parents, Census Bureau Reports." *United States. Census Bureau*. United States Census Bureau, 17 Nov. 2016. Web. 1 Aug. 2017.

SOURCE NOTES
CONTINUED

5. Kim Parker. "Women More Than Men Adjust Their Careers for Family Life." *Pew Research Center*. Pew Research Center, 1 Oct. 2015. Web. 2 Aug. 2017.

6. Christy Lilley. "The Ballad of a Working Mom: Guilt, Anxiety, Exhaustion, and Guilt." *NPR*. NPR, 31 Aug. 2011. Web. 2 Aug. 2017.

7. Joan C. Williams and Rachel Dempsey. *What Works for Women at Work*. New York: New York UP, 2014. Print.

8. Kim Masters. "The To Work or Stay-at-Home Debate." *Parenting*. Meredith Corporation, n.d. Web. 2 Aug. 2017.

CHAPTER 7. UNEQUAL PAY FOR EQUAL WORK

1. Jeanne Sahadi. "Yes, Men Earn More Than Women. Except in These Jobs." *CNN*. Cable News Network, 23 Mar. 2016. Web. 15 Apr. 2017.

2. Ibid.

3. "Federal Poverty Guidelines." *Families USA*. Families USA, Feb. 2017. Web. 2 Aug. 2017.

4. Jonathan Platt, Seth Prins, Lisa Bates, and Katherine Keyes. "Unequal Depression for Equal Work? How the Wage Gap Explains Gendered Disparities in Mood Disorders." *Social Science & Medicine* 149 (2015): 2. Print.

5. "Highlights of Women's Earnings in 2015." *Bureau of Labor Statistics*. U.S. Bureau of Labor Statistics, Nov. 2016. Web. 2 Aug. 2017.

6. Catey Hill. "6 Times It's More Expensive to Be a Woman." *MarketWatch*. MarketWatch, 12 Apr. 2016. Web. 2 Aug. 2017.

7. Mallory Schlossberg. "30 Items That Prove Women Pay More for the Same Products." *Business Insider*. Business Insider, 16 July 2016. Web. 2 Aug. 2017.

8. Catey Hill. "6 Times It's More Expensive to Be a Woman." *MarketWatch*. MarketWatch, 12 Apr. 2016. Web. 2 Aug. 2017.

9. Jonathan Platt, Seth Prins, Lisa Bates, and Katherine Keyes. "Unequal Depression for Equal Work? How the Wage Gap Explains Gendered Disparities in Mood Disorders." *Social Science & Medicine* 149 (2015): 2. Print.

10. Jordan Weissmann. "The Pay Gap Prescription." *Slate*. Slate Group, n.d. Web. 2 Aug. 2017.

11. Ibid.

12. Claire Cain Miller and Liz Alderman. "Why U.S. Women are Leaving Jobs Behind." *New York Times*. New York Times, 12 Dec. 2014. Web. 2 Aug. 2017.

13. "Basic HR Strategies Can Help Close the Gender Gap." *Gale*. Gale, Jan. 2016. Web. 15 Apr. 2017.

14. "The Lifetime Wage Gap, State by State." *National Women's Law Center*. National Women's Law Center, 28 Mar. 2017. Web. 2 Aug. 2017.

15. Sophia A. Nelson. "Equal Pay Day Is Not Equal At All for Women of Color." *HuffPost*. Oath, 4 Apr. 2017. Web. 2 Aug. 2017.

16. "Highlights of Women's Earnings in 2015." *Bureau of Labor Statistics*. U.S. Bureau of Labor Statistics, Nov. 2016. Web. 2 Aug. 2017.

17. "The Lifetime Wage Gap, State by State." *National Women's Law Center*. National Women's Law Center, 28 Mar. 2017. Web. 2 Aug. 2017.

18. "The Simple Truth about the Gender Pay Gap." *AAUW*. AAUW, n.d. Web. 2 Aug. 2017.

19. "The Lifetime Wage Gap, State by State." *National Women's Law Center*. National Women's Law Center, 28 Mar. 2017. Web. 2 Aug. 2017.

20. Geri Stengel. "Why the Force Will Be with Women Entrepreneurs in 2016." *Forbes*. Forbes Media, 6 Jan. 2016. Web. 2 Aug. 2017.

CHAPTER 8. THE GLASS CEILING

1. Madeline Stone. "The Fabulous Life of Facebook Billionaire Sheryl Sandberg." *Business Insider*. Business Insider, 29 July 2014. Web. 2 Aug. 2017.

2. Drew Desilver. "Despite Progress, U.S. Still Lags Many Nations in Women Leaders." *Pew Research Center*. Pew Research Center, 26 Jan. 2015. Web. 2 Aug. 2017.

3. Anna Brown. "The Data on Women Leaders." *Pew Research Center*. Pew Research Center, 17 Mar. 2017. Web. 2 Aug. 2017.

4. Ibid.

5. Julie Hammond. "Financial Services Leadership: Demographics and the Glass Ceiling." *CFA Institute*. CFA Institute, 14 Aug. 2015. Web. 2 Aug. 2017.

6. Dorothy Sue Cobble. *Feminism Unfinished*. New York: Liveright, 2014. Print.

7. "Household Data Annual Averages." *Bureau of Labor Statistics*. Bureau of Labor Statistics, n.d. Web. 2 Aug. 2017.

8. Paula Fernandes. "7 Challenges Women Entrepreneurs Face (and How to Overcome Them)." *Business News Daily*. Purch, 8 Mar. 2017. Web. 2 Aug. 2017.

9. Seth Archer. "Companies with Women in Leadership Roles Crush the Competition." *Business Insider*. Business Insider, 17 June 2016. Web. 2 Aug. 2017.

10. DG McCullough. "Women CEOs: Why Companies in Crisis Hire Minorities—and then Fire Them." *Guardian*. Guardian News and Media Limited, 8 Aug. 2014. Web. 2 Aug. 2017.

11. Christy Glass and Alison Cook. "Leading at the Top: Understanding Women's Challenges above the Glass Ceiling." *The Leadership Quarterly* 27.1 (2016): 51–63. Print.

CHAPTER 9. WHAT'S NEXT FOR WOMEN AT WORK?

1. Dorothy Sue Cobble. *Feminism Unfinished*. New York: Liveright, 2014. Print.

2. Ibid.

3. *MomsRising.org*. MomsRising, n.d. Web. 2 Aug. 2017.

4. Katherine Bowers. "The Juggle Struggle." *Working Mother*. Working Mother, 21 Sept. 2015. Web. 2 Aug. 2017.

5. Chloe Angyal. "Affirmative Action Is Great for White Women. So Why Do They Hate It?" *HuffPost*. Oath, 23 June 2016. Web. 2 Aug. 2017.

6. Jessie Daniels. "White Women and Affirmative Action: Prime Beneficiaries and Opponents." *Racism Review*. Racism Review, 11 Mar. 2014. Web. 2 Aug. 2017.

7. Joan C. Williams and Rachel Dempsey. *What Works for Women at Work*. New York: New York UP, 2014. Print.

8. Ibid.

9. 'Abdu'l-Bahá, *Promulgation of Universal Peace*. Wilmette, Ill: Bahá'í Publishing, 2012. Print.

INDEX

ABOUT THE AUTHORS

DUCHESS HARRIS, JD, PHD

Professor Harris is the chair of the American Studies Department at Macalester College. The author and coauthor of four books (*Hidden Human Computers: The Black Women of NASA* and *Black Lives Matter* with Sue Bradford Edwards, *Racially Writing the Republic: Racists, Race Rebels, and Transformations of American Identity* with Bruce Baum, and *Black Feminist Politics from Kennedy to Clinton/Obama*), she has been an associate editor for *Litigation News*, the American Bar Association Section's quarterly flagship publication, and was the first editor-in-chief of *Law Raza Journal*, an interactive online race and the law journal for William Mitchell College of Law.

She has earned a PhD in American Studies from the University of Minnesota and a Juris Doctorate from William Mitchell College of Law.

GAIL RADLEY

Gail Radley is the author of 25 books for young people and numerous articles for adults. She also teaches part-time at Stetson University in DeLand, Florida, where she lives and cheers on independent, achieving women and girls whenever she can.